CONTENTS

WHAT IS CLIMATE CHANGE?

Our weather is always changing! It can change from season to season, day to day, or even by the hour.

The average weather in a place over many years is called the **climate**. This can also change.

Today, our climate is changing quickly because of the way we live, with worldwide temperatures rising to dangerous levels.

Governments from around the world are now working together to try and stop climate change.

The world's rainfall is changing. Some places are getting more rain than others.

The climate is changing rapidly. As average temperatures rise, we are seeing other changes to the world around us.

These changes include storms becoming more frequent and powerful, an increase in wild fires in hot areas, and **desert** areas are growing in size.

The warmer climate also means that the **polar ice caps** and **glaciers** are melting, causing sea levels to rise.

BURNING FOSSIL FUELS

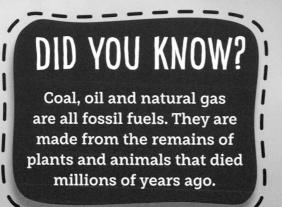

DID YOU KNOW?

Coal, oil and natural gas are all fossil fuels. They are made from the remains of plants and animals that died millions of years ago.

What is causing these changes to happen more quickly?

In the last fifty years, the number of vehicles that people use has grown. Many more factories and power stations have also been built.

Most of these are powered by burning **fossil fuels.** When fossil fuels are burned, a gas called **carbon dioxide** is released.

Scientists believe that releasing more carbon dioxide is making our planet warm up.

More traffic is releasing more carbon dioxide.

The Sun warms the Earth. Then, the Earth warms the layer of gases that surround it. These gases are called the **atmosphere.**

Some gases in the atmosphere, such as carbon dioxide, trap the Sun's heat, like the glass in a gardener's greenhouse. They are known as **greenhouse gases.**

Without these gases, the world would be too cold for living things.

However, an increase in gases, like carbon dioxide, can cause too much heat to be trapped. This leads to **global warming.**

If too many of the greenhouse gases are trapped, the temperature could become too warm.

DID YOU KNOW?

There is more carbon dioxide in the atmosphere today than there has been at any point in the last 800,000 years.

GREENHOUSE GASES

The Sun's heat is absorbed by the Earth.

Some heat is reflected back into space, but now too much is being trapped by the atmosphere.

The rise of global temperatures can have many far reaching effects to the world around us.

Global warming could lead to more extreme weather, including **heat waves**, **droughts** and severe storms. These changes will have a big effect on many people's lives.

It's not just humans that will be affected by global warming. Changes to the climate and weather can affect, and even destroy, the **habitats** of many plants and animals.

GLOBAL WARMING

DID YOU KNOW?

More rainfall from hurricanes and other violent storms could mean more flooding.

MELTING ICE

1979

2000

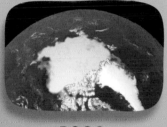

2020

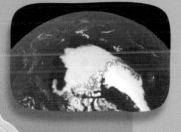

One effect of a warmer world is that ice on mountains and in the Arctic and Antarctic will melt. Changes are already happening.

In the Arctic, a large area of the ocean is frozen all year round. This is called the 'ice cap'. In winter, the ocean around the ice cap freezes too. However, less of it is freezing every year.

If the ice and snow on land in the polar regions melts, sea levels will rise. This will cause flooding to many places around the world.

Satellite photographs show the frozen parts of the ocean in the Arctic shrinking over time.

DID YOU KNOW?

The melting ice could cause polar bears in the Arctic to starve, as it makes it harder for them to hunt.

When Hurricane Katrina hit New Orleans in 2005, the city was flooded.

Melting ice and snow is the best-known cause of rising sea levels, but there is another factor that could raise the level of our oceans.

When water warms up, it expands (gets bigger). Higher temperatures will warm the oceans and seas, causing their waters to expand, and sea levels to rise.

If that were to happen, coastal cities, such as London, New York and New Orleans, could be flooded.

Scientists believe that, because of global warming, some places will have less rainfall in the future. This, combined with warming temperatures drying up water on land, could lead to droughts.

A drought is a long period of time with little or no rainfall.

During a drought, the soil becomes dry and cracked. Only a few plants can survive. Without plants to nourish the soil, the land may be damaged forever and, in some cases, even become a desert.

Herding animals in one of the dry desert areas of the Atlas Mountains in Morocco.

DROUGHTS AND DESERTS

Grazing animals on dry, damaged land makes the plant life disappear even faster.

The good news is that there are things we can do to slow down climate change.

Trees and other plants absorb carbon dioxide from the air. This can stop greenhouse gases from building up in the atmosphere.

The Earth's **rainforests** contain millions of trees and plants.

However, too many rainforests are being cut down for wood, or to make space for growing crops.

It is very important to save the rainforest in order to slow down climate change.

HOW RAINFORESTS HELP

North America

Europe

Asia

Africa

South America

Australia

This map shows the Earth's largest rainforests in dark green.

DID YOU KNOW?

This Scarlet Macaw lives in the Amazon rainforest, in South America. They are in danger of becoming **extinct** because their habitat is being destroyed.

It's not too late to help our planet if humans work together with nature.

Allowing trees to grow will help to reduce the amount of carbon dioxide in the air.

Letting nature reclaim land, and creating more green spaces will help the planet.

To help slow down global warming, humans must switch from burning fossil fuels to using cleaner, **renewable** forms of energy.

The Bosco Verticale in Milan is home to 20,000 trees and plants.

DID YOU KNOW?

Vertical forests, created by growing trees and plants on skyscrapers, can help reduce **smog** and produce **oxygen**.

NATURE AND HUMANS

MAKING ELECTRICITY

A lot of the electricity we use comes from power stations that burn fossil fuels. As well as creating greenhouse gases, supplies of fossil fuels are running out.

Here are some different ways to produce renewable electricity that don't create greenhouse gases:

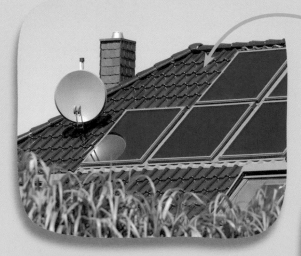

SOLAR POWER

Special panels trap the Sun's energy, which can then be converted into electricity.

HYDRO-ELECTRIC POWER

Moving water creates electricity by turning underwater **turbines**, using the movement of the tide, or water from behind a dam.

WIND POWER

Windmill blades
drive turbines that
make electricity.

GEOTHERMAL POWER

Heat from Earth itself, in
the form of hot water and
steam found underground in
volcanic areas, is converted
into energy.

USE LESS ELECTRICITY

One way we can make a difference to the climate is by using less electricity.

Low energy light bulb

- Use energy saving light bulbs.
- Don't leave electrical items on standby. Turn them off completely when not in use.

- Take showers instead of baths. Showers use less water. Less water means less energy needed to heat it.

Saving water and electricity.

Schools only need energy during the day, so most equipment can be switched off at night.

- Turn down the heating and put on warmer clothes instead.

CHANGING THE WAY YOU TRAVEL

We love to travel around in cars and planes, but they both burn fossil fuels. Planes produce more carbon dioxide than any other form of transport.

- Walk or cycle instead of going by car.

Cycling holidays are becoming more popular.

- Use buses and trains. When lots of people travel together, fewer greenhouse gases are produced per person.

- Electric cars use electricity instead of gas to run. If the electricity to charge them is renewable, they are a great alternative to regular cars because they don't release carbon dioxide!

An electric car being charged.

- Take vacations closer to home so you don't need to fly.

DID YOU KNOW?

So far, the typical electric vehicle battery has been proven to last about 200,000 miles, nearly 20 years.

HOW YOU CAN HELP

TAKE ACTION!

Reuse and recycle! It takes lots of energy to produce packaging, like water bottles and carrier bags. Less energy is needed to make products from recycled material.

Be aware of the electricity you use, and try to reduce it. You could keep an energy journal to help you keep track.

SPREAD THE WORD!

Talk to friends, family and teachers about ways that we can all help to reduce climate change.

atmosphere The air and gases that surround our planet.

carbon dioxide A greenhouse gas given off when things decay or are burnt.

climate Patterns of weather over a long period of time.

desert Dry land with few plants and little rainfall. Deserts are often covered in sand.

drought A long period of time with little or no rainfall, or less rainfall than usual.

extinct When a type of animal or plant no longer exists on Earth.

fossil fuels Fuels such as coal, oil and gas made from the remains of plants and animals that died millions of years ago.

glaciers Huge, slow-moving rivers of ice, often about 100 feet (30 meters) thick. Glaciers move slowly down a slope or valley.

global warming The warming of the Earth's air and oceans because of a build-up of greenhouse gases in the atmosphere.

government A group of people who officially control and make decisions for a country.

greenhouse gases Gases, such as carbon dioxide, that trap warm air in the atmosphere so it cannot escape into space.

heat waves Periods of unusually hot weather.

habitat A place where an animal or plant lives.

oxygen A gas in the air that living things need to breathe.

polar ice caps Large areas of permanently frozen ice in the Arctic Ocean (North Pole) and Antarctic Ocean (South Pole).

rainforests Huge forests of tall trees. Rainforests are normally warm and have lots of rain.

renewable Something that can be replaced and won't run out.

smog A mixture of fog, smoke and chemicals in the air, created by human pollution.

turbine A machine that produces power using fast moving liquids, steam, gas or air.

INDEX